HIDING UNDER THE HEADSET

ENHANCING RESILIENCE FOR TELECOMMUNICATIONS PROFESSIONALS

BY
TANIA GLENN, PSYD, LCSW, CCTP

Progressive
RISING PHOENIX PRESS ®

Text Copyright © 2022 Tania Glenn
All rights reserved.

Published 2022 by
Progressive Rising Phoenix Press, LLC
www.progressiverisingphoenix.com

ISBN: 978-1-950560-90-5

Printed in the U.S.A.

Editor: Jody Amato

Author Photographs: "Tania Glenn" by Jill Hays,
(www.jillhaysphotography.com). Used by permission of the
photographer. © Copyright 2020 Jill Hays.

Cover Design by Kalpart
Visit: www.kalpart.com

Interior design by William Speir
Visit: www.williamspeir.com

Tania Glenn and Arya

Also by Tania Glenn:

First Responder Resilience: Caring for Public Servants

Code Four: Surviving and Thriving in Public Safety

First Responder Families: Caring for the Hidden Heroes

Smashing the Stigma and Changing the Culture in Emergency Services

I've Got Your 6: Peer Support for First Responders

Protected But Scared
(a book for the children of police officers)

This Is Our Normal
(a book for the children of first responders)

To Our Communications Specialists
And to Rowena

Table of Contents

The Story Behind the Documentary

Firepower Resilience: Smashing the Stigma and Caring for First Responders

In 2019, my practice released its first documentary, *First Responder Resilience: Smashing the Stigma.* This documentary highlights seven first responders who faced adversity and received help. I received amazing feedback from first responders all over the country.

In 2021, I decided to release a second documentary that addresses the preventive aspect of what my practice does for first responders. It tells the stories of four first responders who had immediate and rapid intervention from both peer support and my practice, which ultimately led to the mitigation of any further complications caused by the trauma. I believe prevention is a beautiful word and that prevention should be the ultimate goal in trauma care. The dispatcher featured in *Firepower Resilience* is Meghan (featured in the Introduction and also later in the book).

By releasing the documentary, my goals were to help first responders understand the importance of getting good, competent care in a timely manner, to challenge other therapy practices and peer support programs to provide this level of care, and ultimately to give first responders hope.

The documentary was produced by The Visual Brain of Georgetown, Texas. I was excited to find this company, as one of the owners is a Licensed Professional Counselor. The team at The Visual Brain made taking a concept in my mind and turning it into a finished product an easy bridge to cross. Both documentaries can be viewed anytime at:

www.smashingthestigma.com

Foreword

Tania has reached, improved, and certainly saved many lives and countless careers through her practice of combating trauma and building resiliency throughout the public safety and aviation industries. Given that depth of exposure and intimate knowledge of how public safety works, it's no surprise she brings light to the mental health needs of our "first" first-responders, emergency communicators. I've had the pleasure of witnessing and participating in Tania's method of trauma response and resilience building in both a peer support role and as a recipient following traumatic events. Her methodology smashes the stigma of "sitting in a circle and talking about an incident and our feelings…" and really goes after what minds, hearts, and bodies need when faced with trauma or cumulative stress. For those working the front lines of 911 and emergency communications, there is no shortage of stress and trauma—which will only increase as technology advances. It is refreshing to have such a knowledgeable and passionate clinician dedicate time, energy, and attention to our industry of 911 and emergency communications. Read. Absorb. And go build your resiliency!

JC Ferguson
Commander—Austin-Travis Co EMS
Team Leader/Founder—Peer Support

Introduction

It was a Sunday afternoon, and we were standing in Meghan's closet. We were there for one reason—to get her desensitized to wearing her Class A uniform. Nine months earlier, Meghan had been through a worst-case scenario as a dispatcher. She took a 911 call from her best friend's mother. The screams rocked Meghan to the core. Meghan's best friend, Rowena, a fellow dispatcher, had been murdered by her adult son. Not only did Meghan manage through this nightmare call, but she also remained on the radio throughout the four-hour hunt until the perpetrator was found. This was the end to chapter one for Meghan, with many more to follow.

The aftermath for Meghan was brutal. She was intentionally avoiding me because she was afraid to ask for and receive help. I already knew Meghan was a strong individual and that intervening would be challenging. Two days after Rowena's death, when I finally caught up to her, Meghan was standing outside the communications center, crying, shaking uncontrollably, and dry heaving. She had barely slept and was not eating. I handed her my card and told her I would see her the next day.

The healing began, and Meghan started to get her power back. Not only was she able to return quickly to her normal level of functioning, but she also began to flourish in new ways. Meghan started new habits, like making her bed every day. She even became a hard-core daily workout gym devotee.

So here we were, standing in her closet. She had not worn that Class A uniform since Rowena's funeral. She couldn't stand the sight or feel of it. But Meghan had won Employee of the Year at her police department for the second time, and she had to put that uniform on to attend the awards ceremony. To further complicate matters, Meghan's agenda that week not only included the awards ceremony; she was also to attend a Christmas tree lighting honoring the victims of domestic violence, as well as the sneak preview and national release of my practice's documentary, *Firepower Resilience,* that featured Meghan's story. Meghan was facing the type of week that would poke at her resilience, test the effectiveness of her therapy, and challenge her coping skills.

I have always believed that therapy is way more than meeting in an office. It's a process and a work in progress. Sometimes creative healing is the best way to treat a patient. I offered to come to Meghan's house on that Sunday so we could do progressive desensitization to get her in that uniform. I even had a blue finger light in my purse for Eye Movement Desensitization and Reprocessing (EMDR) in case she needed that as well.

We held the uniform on a hanger initially, as we talked about everything—Rowena's life and death, the funeral, the awards ceremony, and the documentary. We decided she should wear something to offset the seriousness of the uniform underneath, so she chose her "Fat Ass Brewery" shirt, complete with a picture of a donkey, to wear below her blouse. It was perfect.

As Meghan pulled that uniform shirt on, we continued to discuss many things. The back-and-forth banter was interspersed with me telling Meghan that she had this, that this was not insurmountable, and that she was a rock star. By the end, Meghan stood there in her shirt, completely unfazed by it, no longer agitated or anxious. She looked at me and said, "I've got this. And you should write a book for communications personnel." As soon as she said this, her closet light timed out and everything went completely dark. We both started laughing and Meghan said, "Apparently God has spoken, too."

I can't think of a better topic for my eighth book. This one is for the communications specialists. You are amazing, and you are loved.

Chapter One

Communications Specialists Are First Responders

I'm a survivor, come ride with me
Been through hell and back, don't need your sympathy
Everything I wanted is right in front of me, yeah
I'm a survivor, come ride with me
"Survivor" by Pop Evil

A few years ago, in my home state of Texas, communications specialists—our dispatchers and 911 call takers—were deemed first responders. To be honest, I was shocked to learn that they were not already considered first responders. I have always addressed police, fire, and emergency medical services (EMS), and in my mind, this also meant the communications professionals who work for these departments. Except for proactive patrol in law enforcement, there is no such thing as public safety without the 911 center. It starts with the call to those three lifesaving and utmost important digits on the telephone. Almost nothing happens without dispatchers and call takers.

For the most part, communications specialists have been considered operators or secretaries for quite a while. A look at some very interesting history reveals why communications specialists have not been considered first responders until recently.

On March 13, 1964, in the very early morning hours, New York City resident Kitty Genovese was attacked with a knife and ultimately murdered just a few blocks from her apartment. The attack lasted several minutes, during which Genovese fought for her life and screamed for help. It was reported that multiple people heard her screams and only one man called the police department. That call went unanswered.

This became a widely known and studied case on human behavior, compassion, and callousness. Additionally, this case is considered one of the driving factors for the development of the emergency 911 call system.

Until the late 1960s, if there was an emergency, people would call the nearest police or fire station, or they would call the operator to get connected to the department they needed. By 1968, the 911 number was established. These numbers were chosen because there were only three, and they were easy to remember. Also, the numbers 911 had not been used as an area code yet.

Initially, those answering 911 calls and dispatching emergency services personnel were typically secretaries. They would answer the call and then pass their notes on to the responding agencies. This explains why those in the profession were classified clerical for many years.

Over the years, emergency communications have evolved. The technology, training, and the services these specialists provide over the phone and on the radios has morphed into a very complex job. Throughout the evolution, the role of telecommunicators has become one of providing police officers, firefighters, and EMS with vital information that they need in order to respond effectively and safely. They also direct the public on what to do, based on the information they are getting, until the members of the field arrive.

Still, somehow, our telecommunications professionals have had to fight for their status as first responders. Perhaps it is the fact that they remain in one place versus going to the scene and they do not interact face-to-face with the public. Perhaps it has simply been the "out of sight, out of mind" problem that our communications personnel have faced since the beginning of the profession. Whatever the reason, it is time for all fifty states to recognize our telecommunications professionals as first responders. Simply by looking at what our communications members do day to day, one can see that they are not operators, secretaries, or clerks.

Ask any field personnel to tell you about their favorite dispatcher. They will tell you that this person feeds them vital information without the need to ask for it, they seem to predict what the field first responders need sometimes before they even realize they need it, and they constantly check on their status to assure their safety. If you probe deeper, many members of the field will tell you that their favorite dispatcher was the voice of calm and reason on their worst day or even that this person saved their life.

Ask any dispatcher how they know someone in the field is in trouble and they will describe very intricate details such as the tone of their colleague's voice, the fact that they keyed up and said nothing or simply the way they keyed up on the radio. The synergy and camaraderie that occur between the field and communications specialists are not only amazing, but also vital to the safety of all personnel. If someone in the field is in trouble, dispatchers stand at the ready to launch the swarm of backup until the situation is stabilized.

In the mid-1990s, a paramedic named Mike was on the ambulance dock at the hospital where I worked as an emergency room social worker at the time. He was restocking his ambulance after a call. His partner was inside the emergency room, completing his paperwork. Just before midnight, a local man with a significant history of mental illness walked up behind Mike and shoved something sharp into his back. The sharp object and the man's hand were covered by a towel and Mike could not tell what it was. The man demanded to be taken to another hospital.

As Mike and the mentally ill man climbed into the ambulance, Mike hit the emergency transponder on his radio to let his beloved dispatchers know that he was in trouble. The communications team responded right away by checking the status and welfare of the crew. Mike's partner, who had no idea any of this was going on, told them they were clear. The dispatcher asked them to reset the emergency transponder. After a few seconds that seemed to last a lifetime, Mike's out-of-breath partner keyed up in complete panic and stated that he was standing on the dock, watching his partner and an unknown occupant drive away in their ambulance.

What ensued next was absolute chaos. This event happened before we had the luxury of the amazing tool known as Global Positioning System, or GPS. This was a time when we still had maps and map books. Communications notified the police department and the rest of the EMS agency immediately. Law enforcement was frantic and so were the rest of the paramedics, many of whom attempted to aid in the search. The problem was that all the ambulances in the same system look identical except for one number on the side and back of the ambulance. It made for a chaotic search for Mike, as ambulances were driving all around looking for him and the police officers were having to figure out that each ambulance they came across was not Mike's.

Meanwhile, Mike smartly drove his abductor to the next closest hospital. The man, in the passenger seat, aimed the weapon, under the towel, at Mike the entire time as he also threatened to kill him. When Mike turned in toward the emergency room at the new hospital, the man jumped out of the ambulance and disappeared. Mike walked into the ER and called the communications center to let them know where he was and that he was okay. He later found the weapon, a screwdriver, as well as the towel, but the abductor was never identified.

Needless to say, the commander on duty asked me to visit the crew that night. As I was getting dressed, I asked what station I should head to, and the request from Mike and his partner was to meet them at IHOP. I have always maintained that we start intervening in every crisis at the base of Maslow's Hierarchy of Needs, which is food, water, clothing, shelter, and safety. So IHOP it was—where we could add caffeine and sugar to the hierarchy of needs.

Sure enough, when I got to the restaurant, the coffee was flowing, the pancakes were smothered in whipped cream, and the entire restaurant had heard the story. So much for confidentiality. If there is one thing I have learned in thirty years of practice with first responders, it's to just go with the flow. As I sat down in the booth, the waitress was calling

Mike "Sugar" and telling him that his meal was on the house.

Mike, his partner, and I chatted it up for a while. They were both coming off the adrenaline rush, but they were both doing remarkably well. In actuality, they were completely good to go.

We all knew, though, that the dispatchers were probably not as good, given the nature of what happened and the fact they were not having the luxury of an IHOP-infused closure. So, we made a plan. We ordered food for me to take to them, and I asked Mike to give me a thirty-minute head start. I went to the communications center and the team started to spill. They talked about the stress of the event and how worried they were throughout the search for Mike's ambulance. As we talked and ate, they started to decompress. I normalized their reactions and educated them on what would be ahead for them. As I wrapped up, Mike walked into the communications center, and it felt like Christmas morning. There were hugs, tears, laughter, and more hugs.

This event highlights some very important points. The first and most important is the absolute cohesion and camaraderie that occurs between the field and communications. They are one team, and they impact each other every day. While Mike's situation resolved itself, the rest of the field and the communications professionals were right there and would have been on top of the situation should it have gone differently. The second point is the fact that our communications personnel are not somehow immune to stress simply because they do not see what is going on. In some cases, it's worse for them because they cannot jump in and help or because they may not have the same level of closure that the field has. The third point is that with every incident, we must consider, remember, and support our telecommunications professionals. To leave them out is to potentially cripple a very important part of every team.

Finally, it is important to address the investment that communications personnel place in the safety of the members of the field. Many still envision the communications center as a separate entity from the field, which is a mistake. Communications centers are the thread that ties the incident together with the field. The communications specialists link the event and the real-time intelligence to the field so they can safely and properly respond. Communications specialists are just as much a part of the team as anyone else, and they take their role, especially when it comes to protecting the field, very seriously.

In 2014, I responded to a very traumatic helicopter crash. On my fifth and final visit to the city where the crash occurred, twenty-six days after the event, my final job was to do progressive desensitization for the flight nurse involved in the incident, which meant getting back in the aircraft and going for a confidence flight. We were at the base, set to go, when in walked four individuals from the communications center. If looks could kill, I'd be dead. The hostility was palpable. I completely understood that they had no idea who I was and that this nurse was their crew member, not mine.

At some point, the four communications team members went into the hangar for a discussion. I heard one of them saying, "I don't know who she is, I don't know who she thinks she is, and I am not sure if I like her." Clearly my smiles and attempts to engage in small talk were not enough.

When they returned to the crew quarters, I knew I had to win them over. They were standing behind a couch staring at me, so I went over to the couch and, rather than sitting down, I put my knees onto the cushions so that I was kneeling and faced the back of the couch. This had me facing them, lower than they were, which was a total act of submission on my part. I am tall, so approaching them and standing close could potentially be threatening, especially given the angst they had about me. As I knelt below their eye level on the couch, I started talking about peer support. I mentioned that the company had given me the green light to schedule training and stand up a peer support team. Then I asked them to join.

"What is peer support?" asked the communications specialist who was talking about me in the hangar. I started to describe what peer support is and how teams operate. I told them how I viewed communications as a vital part of every team, not only for their colleagues in communications, but also for the field. I watched them soften. I knew helping others was the way into their hearts simply by watching how protective they were of the flight nurse. This is the truth of emergency communications. They hold themselves responsible for the field.

By the end of the day, after the confidence flight, we were all hugging each other. They became very dedicated peer support team members. Now we look back and laugh about the first time we met.

Here is a picture from the day we met. As I was writing this book, they sent it to me and told me they were still full of all kinds of funny. I absolutely adore these amazing people.

Chapter Two

The Challenges They Face

Hold, hold on, hold onto me
'Cause I'm a little unsteady
A little unsteady
"Unsteady" by X Ambassadors

Whenever I hire a new therapist, I send them to ride along with the field personnel as well as spend time in communications as often as possible during their first year with the practice. I truly believe that no therapist can treat first responders if they have not ridden out. The experience enriches their skills as a therapist more than any clinical supervision or continuing education ever will.

When my team members come back from their communications ride along, the resounding sentiment is "Wow!" Everyone on my team has the same takeaways—they are amazed at how fast things move, they are extremely impressed with the professionalism that communications specialists maintain, they all have a headache from the experience, and they all want to go back for another ride along because they want to learn more.

The challenges that our communications specialists face are numerous, and these challenges can and do impact the overall health of these professionals. While the challenges of any communications center can be numerous, this chapter focuses on the impact of the work to the hearts and minds of our dispatchers and 911 call takers, which is my specialty. Chapter Four will address the solutions, but first let's start with the challenges.

Ergonomics and Shift Work

Many communications centers have evolved into state-of-the-art, highly advanced workplaces that provide the latest technology, noise control, and comfort. However, there are still many communications centers across the country that have not received the funding for such advances. Either way, the challenges remain.

One of the most significant challenges that dispatchers and 911 call takers face is long shifts with long stretches of time where they cannot move around. Communications specialists cannot leave in the middle of a call or take a break when things are busy. Many communications specialists report that they frequently skip meals and do not use the restroom for twelve hours, depending on how busy the shift is.

Sitting at a console, unable to move or take a break, and dealing with high-stress incidents, means the generation of the stress hormone cortisol for communications specialists, with no way to work it out of their systems. High cortisol production is associated with high stress. The brain and body do this to protect the person, and it is ultimately meant for the stressful moment and not as a continual, long-term response.

During high stress, the cortisol receptors in each cell will use cortisol to shut down functions that might not be necessary at the time, such as digestive and reproductive systems, the immune system and growth processes. This function is meant to be a short-term, occasional process to help the brain and body through a high-stress incident, with the goal to return to normal as quickly as possible.

But what happens when the alarm button is continually pushed? Communications specialists dealing with high volumes of stressful calls—shift after shift—are in constant cortisol production. When this happens, many body functions become derailed, and the impact on one's health is massive. Chronically high cortisol levels have been associated with depression, anxiety, weight gain, memory loss, difficulty concentrating, heart disease, headaches, and problems with digestion and sleeping.

In order to combat the high cortisol levels from such a high-stress occupation, communications specialists must engage in the activities that build resilience—eat right, exercise, get enough rest, practice their hobbies, and reduce their caffeine intake. When someone shows this list of cortisol-busting strategies to most communications specialists, they will likely respond with dismay and frustration. A list like this may be too overwhelming and seem like a full-time job in addition to the one they already have, not to mention the rest of their lives that they must manage, including their families. In Chapter Four, I will address the ways to feasibly manage resilience building to improve health.

The other ergonomic challenge that communications personnel face is the fact that they sit at a console, look from screen to screen, and type all shift. If the chairs and keyboards are outdated, the likelihood of improper ergonomic positioning can cause strain and overuse injuries.

During high-stress calls, many communications specialists will switch from sitting in the ergonomically healthy L position to leaning forward, straining their shoulders and pulling their feet off the floor into what is essentially a crouched position. Unless a communications specialist realizes they are doing this and consciously resets their position, they will maintain this crouch for hours. At the end of the shift, they are completely sore from the strain of this position.

The fact that communications specialists cannot switch tasks and move around, denies them the ability to reset their bodies and eliminate overuse fatigue. The nature of the job simply does not allow for this. Ultimately, this leads to fatigue, stress, and discomfort, which will impact the moods of most communications specialists.

Shift work is another issue for public safety, including communications personnel. There is much research on the impact of shift work and this topic is an entire book in and of itself. For communications personnel, as with other professions, shift work is associated with higher stress levels, job dissatisfaction, and poor mental and physical health.

While there is no way around shift work for communications personnel, the key is to balance the drain of shift work with each person's resilience and life outside of the job. Twelve-hour shifts are a long haul and can be very draining, but they afford more days off, which many communications professionals value. The key is to restore balance and resilience on those days off, along with everything else that needs to get done. What I ask our dispatchers and 911 call takers to consider is the fact that we all have an internal fuel tank. The nature of public safety work drains that internal fuel tank, so on days off, each professional must make time to refuel that internal fuel tank so they can return to work with a full tank. More on this later.

Dealing with the Public

No one calls 911 because they are having a good day. The nature of a 911 call is never fun, pleasant, or happy. Public safety professionals interact with the public on the worst days of their lives, are subject to horror, chaos, violence, illness, despair, death, and the victimization of the innocent. It all starts with the 911 call, where a dispatcher must quickly assess, intervene, and manage a situation with the limitations of a phone interaction.

Any first responder in the field who gripes about the way the dispatchers do their job should spend a shift under a headset. What they will quickly learn is that dealing with these calls is far more convoluted than they probably think. When people call 911, they are in shock, afraid, confused, and traumatized. Sometimes they are under the influence of drugs or alcohol. Frequently they cannot figure out where they are, much less what to do. Sometimes they are speaking other languages. Frequently those who call 911 are screaming, yelling, talking extremely fast, or crying. Sometimes they are abusive, degrading, or just disgusting on the phone. Regardless of what is happening with a caller, call takers must stay on the line until the bridge has been made to the field.

Dispatchers face each shift with the lack of predictability of what will happen that day. While part of the appeal is that the calls and the shifts are never the same, there is always an underlying sense or worry that maybe today will be the day when a call is too overwhelming.

When the call comes in, dispatchers and 911 call takers must take control of the situation by directing and redirecting the caller so that they can gain as much information as possible to send to the field. Each time they interact with a caller, there is always a risk associated with not getting enough information or not detecting an urgent situation and therefore not passing enough information on to the field. They must make multiple decisions very quickly, all while multitasking and controlling their emotions and in an environment with significant background noise, either in the communications center or on the other end of the call.

The Boredom-to-Chaos Rollercoaster

As with the rest of public safety, communications personnel must also balance and manage the times when the system is slow and, despite the low call volume, dispatchers and 911 call takers must remain vigilant. At a moment's notice, everything can change. Remaining vigilant is essential to the work of any public safety professional.

Balancing the slow times and boredom with maintaining vigilance, knowing that anything can happen at any time, is both a physical and a psychological drain for first responders. Communications professionals leave their shifts experiencing the same adrenaline dumps as those in the field do. Their brains and bodies activate to be ready for everything for the duration of the shift, and when they are on their way home, their brains pull the plug on this activation, and they experience the same parasympathetic nervous system backlash, or adrenaline dump, that police officers, firefighters, and paramedics do. When they walk into their homes, they are just as exhausted, numb, impatient, and checked out as the members of the field are.

In my book *First Responder Families: Caring for the Hidden Heroes*, I address the impact of shift work and fatigue on both first responders and their families. This obviously includes communications professionals. Below is an excerpt from the book.

> *A chief complaint from first responder family members is how significant the impact of shift work is on their home lives. Public safety personnel walk through the doors of their homes*

at the end of their shifts completely drained. Their internal fuel tanks are on a solid E for empty, and they are completely void of energy, patience, and a desire to do anything other than sleep or stare at the TV. This happens to coincide with a time when the family may be ready to run errands, get chores done, or for parents, even take a break from dealing with very young children. They've been waiting for their first responder to walk through the front door. It is a perfect mismatch of expectations and energy levels, all under one roof, all at the same time. This is a tough thing to navigate, given how busy lives can be with the demands of schedules and high expectations that we have for each other.

The key to managing this is to find your family rhythm through navigating the impact of shift work on first responders and finding the happy medium between an empty internal fuel tank and the needs of a busy family system. In other words, acknowledge and understand the mismatch of energy and life rhythm, and work through it.

The first thing to understand is the impact of shift work on first responders. As the uniform goes on toward the beginning of the shift, first responders typically are focused on what's ahead. They may be watching the news, listening to their work radio, or checking in with on-duty crews. As they head out the door, safety and non-complacency become the priority. In order to do this, situational awareness is vital. Everything in a worst-case scenario boils down to being prepared, muscle memory, and training. Being caught off guard or behind the curve during a dangerous incident is every first responder's worst nightmare.

What this means is that most first responders are already in what I call a "low-grade fever level of fight or flight" before they even leave the house. Their bodies have already started producing more adrenaline, glucose, and cortisol as they hit the streets or enter their stations. Throughout the shift, as calls come in, first responders will ride the fight-or-flight wave throughout the duration of their duty time. If a certain call is dangerous

23

or extremely difficult, public safety personnel can and will enter full-blown fight or flight and maintain it for as long as they need to.

Because they are riding the fight-or-flight wave throughout a shift, first responders tend to feel great. They are energized, witty, and happy. This is short-lived, because the brain and body will only maintain this for as long as it needs to.

At the end of the shift, on the drive home, first responders hit the adrenaline "dump." As the brains of first responders determine that they are safe, they tell the body to let off the fight-or-flight response because it is no longer necessary. For most first responders, this occurs as they are pulling into their neighborhood or when they are about three miles from their home if they live in a rural area.

As your first responder is walking in the door, their energy is crashing. They will comment about how tired they are, how they don't want to make any decisions, how they want to be left alone. This is an actual physical withdrawal they are going through, and it is just as much a part of every shift as the ramp-up is when they are on their way to work.

For family members, this is not fun or easy to navigate. Families frequently express frustration about how energized and happy their first responder is at work and how angry and withdrawn they are at home. Family members are on the receiving end of grumpy, withdrawn, depressed, and angry first responders.

The key here is to not take this personally and to allow for the necessary rebound or rally time that your first responder needs. This means that, as a couple, you communicate about the best way to navigate through this cycle.

The historical tendency has been to downplay the stressors faced by our communications specialists. "They don't actually go to the calls" has been a damaging attitude that has minimized what communications specialists experience on the job. Looking at the science of stress, what happens to the brain and the body, shift work, ergonomics, and the nature of emergency services work, it is easy to see that downplaying or minimizing the stress our dispatchers and 911 call takers experience is a drastic mistake.

Call to Call

Finally, it is important to address the fact that the nature of emergency services can be one extreme to another. When the system is busy, the calls take priority over taking a break or self-care for all emergency service workers, and this certainly includes communications specialists.

Consider the impact of taking the most horrendous type of call, where a parent kills their child while on the phone. Then think about going from that call to one where a person is complaining about where their neighbor parked their car or placed their trash can. When a system is busy, it leaves little to no time for communications specialists to begin to process the very traumatic calls they may have sustained.

With traumatic calls comes sensory overload, a fight-or-flight response, and a complete physical and psychological activation of the body's defense mechanisms. No human being can shut this activation off like a switch because the human brain cannot make the transition from a fight-or-flight response without a recovery period. Yet somehow, we expect our dispatchers and 911 call takers to switch from one extreme to another, and somehow to switch off the caveman amygdala portion of the brain that was engaged in the fight-or-flight response, and that is still firing away in their brain after a traumatic call.

Communications specialists are very good at speaking evenly and calmly. It is a skill they develop over time. Their words are measured with firmness and concern. As soon as they sit down at the console, the communications specialist voice turns on. Radio disc jockeys do the same thing. I have noticed during radio interviews that DJs have a radio voice and their normal, natural voice. Communications specialists have the same.

I firmly believe when people complain about the behavior of a first responder who does not generally garner complaints, the first question supervisors must ask is, "What changed or what happened in this person's life?" When the public complains about the tone or rudeness of a communications specialist, supervisors should look at two things.

The first is the current circumstances in that person's life causing significant stress and the second is the call history for that communications specialist on that shift and even from the past several shifts. A simple pause with a good assessment of the situation can lead to much better methods of addressing problems that arise in the workplace.

A few years ago, I posted this article on my practice's social media. It is such a glaring example of what happens when departments punish first responders after trauma without asking the simple question, "What changed or what happened?"

"Please Stop Throwing Away First Responders"

I recently did EMDR on a veteran police officer. On a day when he responded to a significantly traumatic incident where he saved lives and demonstrated behaviors that would have resulted in a valor award, he ended up in legal trouble after behaving in an uncharacteristic manner. Not only does he not remember engaging in this behavior or what he was thinking or feeling during that time, what he did was not anything he had ever done before or would have ever dreamed of doing.

The aftermath of this event included being terminated from his department. No one took the time to explore why his behavior changed so drastically after a huge trauma. No one took the time to ask, "What happened?"

So, what did happen? First off, when he launched into fight or flight to run into a very dangerous situation and save multiple lives, his heart rate likely hit 180 beats per minute and his prefrontal cortex (the portion of the brain in charge of thinking, reasoning, analyzing, memory management, fine motor skills, math, and the rest of those higher human cognitive functions) basically shut down while his amygdala (the caveman who kicks butt and takes names) turned on. He went into total fight mode, was strong, felt no pain, and did what he had to do to help others in the most heroic fashion possible. Later that day, he reported feeling agitated, angry, and aggressive. This is because his amygdala was still firing away. Then, after many hours of fight mode, this officer was sent home at the end of the sixteen-hour activation to begin to attempt to return to normalcy.

He reported feeling numb, agitated, and restless that night, even though he was exhausted. This is because he was experiencing the adrenaline "dump" or the parasympathetic nervous system backlash that happens after fight-or-flight activations. He reported being in a fog and not realizing he was behaving strangely because it takes the prefrontal cortex about two nights with at least somewhat decent sleep to turn back on.

Ultimately this officer engaged in risky behavior, was terminated, and bounced around for years before he landed in his current department. The years, of course, included pain, financial difficulties, and interpersonal problems.

And then there is the rest of the story. One session of EMDR brought about the fact that as a child, he went through a very similar trauma to the one he had experienced on duty that day. So not only was he in fight-or-flight mode with a prefrontal cortex turned off and a fully engaged caveman amygdala on, the internal buttons created by this childhood trauma—every last one of them—were pushed that day.

Yet somehow the department expected this officer to be just fine, to not have any issues after the event, and to return to normal duty accordingly. And this is true for thousands of departments across the country. So often, unrealistic expectations coupled with little or poor psychological care create the perfect storm for behavioral and psychological problems in first responders after trauma.

None of this knowledge of the stress response is new. None of it is earth-shattering, breaking news. Yet somehow, we continue to fail our first responders by isolating, punishing, and criticizing them. Leadership comments that a person has changed. Why not, instead, ask someone, "What happened?" or "What changed?" Maybe they won't know right away, but why not take the time to find out? Why not make the effort to get them help?

In no way am I saying that there should not be consequences for bad behavior. Certain

> *behaviors are inexcusable, and termination is sometimes necessary. With this officer who had no history of any complaints or discipli-nary actions, he could have bounced back with a probationary period and some good trauma care. He would have most likely pro-ceeded in his career with wisdom and the type of experience he could pay forward by helping other officers.*

In my most recent book, *Code Four: Surviv-ing and Thriving in Public Safety*, I challenge leadership and first responders to make the commitment to care for personnel rather than throwing them away. These are the final words in my book and I absolutely see this every day:

> *First responders DO recover from burnout, trauma, and PTSD. They return to the line with wisdom and resilience. They make some of the best employees you will ever have the privilege of leading, because they understand themselves and others. After recovering from trauma, first responders have more compas-sion, patience, and insight. They become ex-*

perts in handling the public and in looking out for their fellow first responders. We call this post-traumatic growth. The magic words I hear in my office every day as people achieve post-traumatic growth: "I wouldn't wish this on anyone, but this experience has made me better, stronger, and wiser." We should all be so lucky to have first responders on our team who have reached post-traumatic growth.

In my book *Smashing the Stigma and Changing the Culture in Emergency Services,* I highlight and contrast two highly traumatic events sustained by first responders. Both received care and ultimately healed, but one was punished with no consideration for what had occurred, while the other was assessed and helped by his peer support team and sent to my practice for care. The journeys these two individuals took toward healing were very similar, except for the support and culture of their respective departments. At the end of the healing process, the support or lack thereof from a department can impact a person's attitude and performance for a long time, if not permanently.

Bryce's Story

Bryce is an amazing dispatcher with the Cedar Park Police Department. He is a survivor of the Route 91 Harvest Festival active shooter incident, and this story is featured in my book *Smashing the Stigma and Changing the Culture in Emergency Services*. Two days before Bryce's interview about surviving the Route 91 incident, this event happened. While I could not interview him at the time for legal reasons, here is another amazing story from Bryce.

August 16, 2020, started out as most Sundays do. Hot Texas heat and a slow day in the communications center. Slow Sundays are far from unusual in our city of Cedar Park, which is just under 100,000 people. Like most dispatch centers, we were understaffed. The minimum for the day shift is four people and three on weekends if we just can't get someone to pick up the overtime. This was one of those days.

I was working the police dispatch radio. My supervisor, Nicholle, was working the fire dispatch radio and a trainee, Ashley, was working phones. Ashley was able to work phones because she had passed that part of training. The day was slow. So slow that around 2 p.m., I started throwing gummy worms up in the air and trying to catch them in my mouth. Embarrassing, yes, but true story. A gummy worm hit the ground, so I put a napkin over it and held a mini funeral. That's how slow this day was going. The kind of day where time just stands still.

Unbeknownst to us, at around 3:11 p.m., time would literally stand still as the dreaded words echoed through the radio, "Officers down."

The originating event was a call from a mother who said her son stole her vehicle and was mentally unstable. When officers responded, the son was no longer on scene and no one was answering the door to the residence. So, the officer left. About twenty minutes later, the mother was back on the line, advising her son had returned and was trying to break into the house. With officers enroute, the caller was locking herself and two other kids in the upstairs bedroom. The caller opened her bedroom door and said her son was in the house and possibly had a weapon.

When officers arrived, they found the front door barricaded. At this time, the caller began to scream that the male had made entry into her room. Officers entered the house, where they were met with gunfire. As we listened to gunfire erupt on the phone, the officers called out, "Shots fired!" Immediately following an officer keyed up, advising an officer had been shot, followed by "I've been shot," followed by "We have three officers hit."

My coworkers started to break down and cry. Both for different and valid reasons. Ashley was so new, she had never experienced something like this before. Niki, because of her many years with the department, felt an attachment to the officers and we didn't know their statuses. I was firm with my coworkers and said, "Get it together and stop crying and focus on getting the job done. We can cry later." Being a survivor of the Route 91 Harvest Festival shooting, I knew the best thing we could do was to stay calm.

We had just about every agency around Central Texas responding to us. We called neighbors nearby to advise them to shelter in place, explaining the side of the house where they should shelter for their utmost safety. We determined the staging location for fire and EMS, as well as the command center. It went from one of the slowest days to the most hectic day in my entire career.

Thankfully, all our officers survived that day. The communications center had supervisors and other dispatchers here within twenty minutes to help field calls. Like most dispatchers, I felt like I had to finish out my shift before I could hand it over. Whenever anyone would come into the room, I couldn't look at them because I knew I would start crying. I just stared at my screen and did my job.

After the event was over, everyone continued to check in on each other, just to make sure we were all okay. Our members of command staff came in and gave amazing words of affirmation and acknowledgement. We went through it together and we came out of it together. But it was a good re-minder of how everything can change in literally a few seconds.

Bryce

Chapter Three

Communications Trauma

Reaching out, give me a lifeline
I don't know if I can carry this on my own
Living lost can last a lifetime
I don't know if I can carry this on my own
"Lifeline" by Bad Wolves

At any given time in my practice, communications personnel are consistently between 25 and 30 percent of our patient population. This is good and bad. It's good because it means communications professionals recognize the need to get help, and they are asking for it. It's bad because it's a strong indicator of the stress and trauma our dispatchers and 911 call takers are going through.

Trauma

Trauma happens through the five senses—what we see, hear, taste, touch, and smell. This information enters the frontal lobe of our brains. When this information is normal and nontraumatic, the frontal lobe passes it off to our prefrontal cortex, which decides what will happen to it—either it goes to short-term or long-term memory, depending on relevance.

During traumatic events, this information flow is completely disrupted. What we see, hear, taste, touch, and smell is captured by the frontal lobe to deal with later. The reason the frontal lobe captures this information is because the person sustaining the trauma is way too busy—surviving, fighting, fleeing or, in the case of emergency communications, working to resolve the situation. For first responders, training and muscle memory kick in while emotional numbing is fully engaged to keep that first responder in the moment and capable of doing their job. At the same time the frontal lobe is capturing the information, the prefrontal cortex has shut down, as this is a physiological side effect of the heart rate hitting 180 beats per minute during stress.

In the aftermath of a traumatic event, the replay begins. What the first responder saw, heard, tasted, touched, and smelled comes back as though it's a video in their mind. For most first responders, this starts when things really calm down or during the drive home. The replay continues—in the shower, watching TV, having dinner with family, during sleep (as nightmares), and even into the next day.

In my practice, with the creation of the concept we call "firepower resilience," we have created a new protocol for our customers after trauma. What we ask all our first responders to do is to keep their fingers on their psychological pulse after a trauma. The guidelines we give are as follows: for the first few days after the event, it is completely normal to replay the event a lot and to have nightmares about it. By seven days post-incident, we want our first responders to describe the event as though it is starting to fade. In other words, the replay has slowed down, ideally the nightmares have stopped, and first responders are feeling as though they are returning to normal. By fourteen days post-incident, we want the event banked in their long-term memory. We explain that at this point, the first responder will still think about the event, but not like they did during the first few days after the incident.

The best word we use to describe this experience is fading—the healthy resilient brain will move the sights, smells, sounds, tactile sensations, and tastes from the frontal lobe to the long-term memory because that is what it is designed to do. The difference between a trauma and a bad memory is that a trauma will remain trapped in the frontal lobe and trigger the person until they get help and possibly forever if they don't. A bad memory, however, is downloaded and processed, and put into a place that is manageable. We all have bad memories, but the key is we can pull them up, think about them and then tuck them back into our long-term memory without being triggered.

At the fourteen-day mark, we tell our customers to ask for help if they do not have good fading. The reason is two-fold. Most first responders, with all their good training and experience, can successfully bank traumatic calls into their long-term memory. It's when they don't that I begin to worry. The second reason is that if a first responder is reaching out for help at the two-week mark, everything we are doing in therapy is preventative. At the fourteen-day point, a first responder who is still distressed by an event is experiencing post-traumatic stress syndrome. This is a normal reaction to a horrible event, and it is not the end of the continuum, which is post-traumatic stress disorder (PTSD). Getting help when it is still considered syndrome versus disorder is the key. Everything we are doing at this point is prevention. In my opinion, prevention is such a beautiful word, and providing preventative care is the highest level of service we can provide.

Additionally, I always make it clear that the fourteen-day point is a hard outer limit. If someone is struggling, hurting, and miserable, I do not want them to wait for two weeks to see if anything has changed. We all know ourselves. Our family knows us. If it's one day post-incident and you know you are impacted, it is time to initiate help. I would never want anyone to "gut it out" to see if things improve. If you are hurting, please reach out. In Chapter Five, we will address solutions and treatment.

Auditory Trauma

Communications professionals are frequently exposed to auditory trauma. Because they listen to the awfulness of 911 calls, the trauma gets stored as sound. There may not be any images of the event because they did not see it, but auditory trauma is just as bad as visual trauma. Sometimes, it can be worse.

While the field often asks for help in processing images, our dispatchers and 911 call takers ask us to help them process the sounds. The first problem that frequently occurs with auditory trauma is that at times, the sound of something is much worse than it looks. The second problem with auditory trauma is that without a visual, a communications specialist will use their imagination to put the pieces of the puzzle together. What they imagine can be and usually is so much worse than the actual image.

What this means for communications specialists is that they frequently lack closure on situations. If the field does not realize how bad something sounded, there is no way for them to know or realize that a communications specialist may need to hear from them. If a shift is extremely busy, the field may not have time to visit with the dispatchers and 911 call takers. By the end of the shift, they may be too tired or have forgotten to touch base with communications. Many communications specialists will wonder for a very long time or even forever about a certain call. The pervasive stance is that they don't want to bother the field for closure because they are busy or because they don't want to burden them. So, these calls then linger.

I truly believe that the act of closing the loop on unanswered questions—filling in the pieces of the puzzle—for both the field and the communications specialists is an important practice. This brings closure, understanding and, many times, it brings resolution.

During the time early in my career when I worked in an emergency room, the HIPAA rules were implemented nationally. Before HIPAA, paramedics could call the ER to ask how a patient turned out. They did this for closure, because the human brain, in many situations, craves the ability to understand the big picture as well as the outcome. Even if their patient had died, knowing how things turned out and any additional information from the ER would help them learn, develop their skills, and put the call to bed. At the onset of the HIPAA regulations, the answer from the ER quickly became "we can't tell you anything." Some systems still restrict the information, while others have relaxed this with the understanding that the paramedics were the beginning of the patient care. Let us not forget, however, that emergency communications were involved even before the field entered the picture. Let us not forget that many times, communications personnel need that same closure too.

Secondary/Vicarious Trauma

Secondary or vicarious trauma is an indirect experience of, or exposure to, a traumatic event. Hearing a firsthand account of an event will cause secondary trauma. The mantra of secondary trauma in emergency services is, "This did not happen to me, I should not need help." When my patients say this, I explain that as human beings, we absorb the pain of others. Secondary trauma is just as important to address as direct trauma.

Secondary trauma manifests in several ways. Emotionally, a person may experience intense sadness, anxiety, fear, hopelessness, frustration, and guilt. Physically, the symptoms are headaches, stomach upset, and constipation. Cynicism, irritability, and disconnection from others are the interpersonal hallmarks of secondary trauma. Obviously, secondary trauma is a huge factor in turnover.

The main problem with secondary trauma and communications personnel is when leadership does not recognize or understand this. The ability to embrace secondary trauma is just as important as embracing and caring for direct trauma. When a department adopts policies and mechanisms to help dispatchers and 911 call takers with secondary trauma, it normalizes this response to stress and offers solutions.

One of my first patients with secondary trauma was a Navy nurse. On a naval ship, she had cared for a well-known Army aviator who was shot down during the first Gulf War, taken as a prisoner of war, and released a week later. The trauma was extensive and horrible. As they floated home on the Naval ship, this nurse gave her patient the best possible care she could. The aviator went on to have a very successful recovery and career. Many years later, as this nurse sat down on my couch and burst into tears, those words came out of her mouth—"This did not happen to me, I should not need help." After I explained the absolute legitimacy of secondary trauma, we got to work. My nurse patient was able to heal fully and successfully. The first and very important step for her was to identify and understand secondary trauma.

Helplessness and Guilt

Helplessness is one of the most pervasive emotions that gets attached to trauma. The experience of helplessness is extremely negative for the human psyche. Helplessness is the absolute worst emotion in emergency services.

All first responders—communications, police, fire, and EMS—are trained to always stay in control. Public safety personnel are taught to take charge, maintain control, and regain it if it is somehow lost. This mindset is engrained in all the training.

But what happens if you cannot get control or maintain it? What happens when you can't get good information from the caller, can't get people on scene to cooperate, can't get there fast enough, can't get pulses back, and can't change the outcome? While some situations are easy to reconcile because of timelines or other facts such as the time of death being well before the first 911 call, others are not.

The events that ultimately lead to the damaging effects of helplessness are typically the traumatic events that overwhelm those who are exposed, the valiant efforts to change the outcome, and

47

ultimately the inability to do so. These events are typically ones involving children, known victims, and public safety personnel.

In my work with first responders, helplessness is the number-one emotion that is processed during trauma treatment (see Chapter Five). I tell first responders that this emotion, wrapped around a trauma, is like an ugly ogre sitting on your chest breathing fire into your face all the time. Helplessness coupled with trauma is by far the most destructive problem first responders face, in terms of their mental health.

When mental health problems exist, the brain always goes to bad. Think in terms of depression. When depressed people hear voices, those voices don't tell them that today is going to be a better day and to get up and go for a walk. Instead, the voices tell depressed people to kill themselves and, as a matter of fact, everyone around them will be better off if they do it. This could not be further from the truth!

The problem with trauma coupled with helplessness is that the brain once again goes to the bad. Trauma coupled with helplessness tells a person that they failed, that they were not good enough, or that they somehow don't deserve what they have. When this happens, first responders frequently suppress the rest of the story—the valiant efforts they made to change an outcome, the risks they took to their own life in order to attempt to save others, or even the facts of the situation where the outcome was already determined. All of this is extremely damaging to the mental health of first responders.

Helplessness is one of the hallmark emotions for communications personnel. Having to sit through a call or a situation, managing and disseminating as much information as they can, providing other resources, and being the voice of calm and reason is a massively important role during a trauma. However, the most pervasive sentiment that dispatchers and 911 call takers express is the desire to reach through the phone or the console and help the situation. Communications personnel must be allowed to process the helplessness they experience in a safe setting.

Guilt is another hallmark emotion. Dispatching a first responder to a call that results in a line-of-duty death is the absolute worst guilt-provoking event for a dispatcher. This is their worst nightmare and the likelihood of developing post-traumatic stress disorder from such an event is very high if personnel do not get immediate and proper care.

Another guilt-inducing event is when 911 call takers give instructions to the public during a crisis, and even though they give the best information they can based on the protocol they are trained to use, people still die. Again, this is very traumatic for communications professionals, and they need immediate access to competent trauma care.

Survivor guilt is a condition of persistent emotional stress experienced by someone who survived an event while others did not. Survivor guilt is pervasive and awful. It is complex to treat and requires a skilled therapist. Many surrounding those who suffer from survivor guilt will see the guilt as irrational. If there is one way to shut down someone you love, it is to call their guilt irrational.

Survivor guilt is the result of the facts of the situation—the who, what, when, where, and how, coupled with the person's interpretation of the event. The interpretation is frequently one of self-blame because of the outcome. The trauma of the situation, coupled with the person's interpretation, leads to the emotion called survivor guilt.

In May 1997, an F5 tornado struck the town of Jarrell, Texas. This tornado ravaged the town of Jarrell before it hopped over to Cedar Park, Texas, where it crushed a grocery store. It finished its deadly course by hopping over Lake Travis and taking out a trailer park. On the night this happened, I went to work in the trailer park, assisting with death notifications. The next day, I was in Jarrell. I remember standing next to a state trooper and asking him where all the "stuff" was. He asked me to clarify what I meant by "stuff," and I explained that I was wondering where all the overturned vehicles, washing machines, furniture, etc. was. The trooper looked at me and said that the "stuff" was a pile of dust and debris about half a mile away. It was truly awful.

I worked for the next month to assist first responders who responded to the tornado. On day six I was interacting with a 911 call taker when everything seemed to implode. She told me that she took the 911 calls that day, and that per her training she told the callers to remain inside, to get into their bathtubs, and to cover themselves with mattresses. Her interpretation, based on this awful trauma wrapped up in guilt, was that she had killed these people. She kept asking me if she should have told them to run.

She went on to disclose that she had been working nonstop since the event, that she was not sleeping and was not eating. She allowed herself a cup of water each day. When I asked her to consider self-care, she told me that she did not deserve to practice self-care. She was essentially flogging herself for doing her job. This is how quickly and severely survivor guilt can destroy people.

As the alarm bells rang in my head, my amazing peer support team came to the rescue. She continued to talk to me, saying basically the same thing over and over. I told her I was concerned about her being dehydrated. Maslow's Hierarchy of Needs is the language of first responders in a crisis, not feelings or therapeutic interpretations. I always begin with food, water, clothing, and shelter because it is the best way to show someone you care about where they are at this point in their life. She agreed that she was probably dehydrated. I asked her if she would be willing to go to the ER and receive IV fluids to get hydrated again, assuring her she could go back to work later on, and of course hoping she would not. A paramedic and a police officer from the peer support team took her to the hospital and let me know that as soon as the fluids hit her veins, she was asleep. Of course she was. She was exhausted. The ER staff assured my team they would take good care of her and pass her off to her family upon discharge, which they did. Fortunately, this call taker realized how bad off she had been, and she ended up taking some time off and getting help so she could restore her resilience.

For our telecommunications specialists, trauma comes in multiple forms. Their need for care is just as important as anyone in the field. As with any first responder who experiences trauma and gets help, the post-traumatic growth that comes from facing adversity often creates some of the best employees any agency can have.

Dispatchers across the United States sharing their love for each other, their work and the communications community.

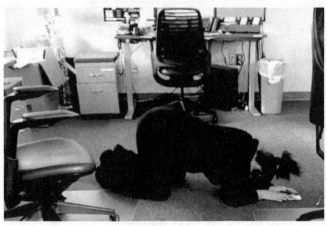

Chapter Four

Solutions

Well I'm not looking back
Because I've become unbreakable
I can feel myself coming alive
'Cause I will fight to overcome
Now that, I am
Unbreakable
"Unbreakable" by Kingdom Collapse

In any high-stress occupation, self-care is of utmost importance to the health and well-being of the individual. While public safety personnel are excellent at caring for others, their self-care is often inadequate.

In my practice, we work diligently to care for first responders from a systems perspective. We see each person as a complex overlay of who they are, their history, what they do, whom they have in their life, what their health is like, what their habits are and, most importantly, whom and what they love. It is important to see a person as a complex overlay of the many facets of their life, so we can garner their strengths to build on them and identify what needs to change so we can help them make adjustments.

Resilience

In therapy, we start with resilience. The word resilience became a hot topic about seven years ago. Agencies were charged with making the workforce resilient. But what does that mean?

I like to think of resilience building as tangible and identifiable steps to take toward self-improvement. Resilience building means a series of minor adjustments, not an overhaul of one's life. We are creatures of habit and creating change is not easy, especially as we get older.

Resilience building is not a New Year's resolution. Statistically, these resolutions are abandoned by the middle of February. Somehow on January 1st we are supposed to commit to a new way of being or to a goal without tangible objectives to reach that goal. The most common resolution is that people want to "lose weight" or "get into shape," whatever that means. So, many people decide to join a gym. The gym companies, meanwhile, are waiting. This is the most profitable time of the year! As you go in to join a gym with the best of intentions, the sales-person will explain that since it's a new year, there is a special. This special is usually something along the lines of saving 30 percent if you pay for the whole year in advance. Saving that much money sounds great, so you hand over your credit card.

What happens next is typically some variation of this scenario: you go twice. You work out too hard the first time, so you are really sore. Then you make yourself go again and you are miserable. Then you look at the pretty people in the locker room who go every day and get frustrated because you don't look like them yet. Then you get a cold from all the germs on the free weights. And then you never go back again. Until the next year.

When I address resilience with a patient, we start with the basics—hydration, nutrition, rest, and exercise. We set tangible goals and objectives to reach those goals. For example, adding eight ounces of water to your day and adding one hundred steps to your day (fitness trackers are great for this). Then, a week or two later, we add sixteen ounces of water to your day and two hundred steps. This is how we start to create change.

I often tell people during the early stages of resilience building, since you are changing your habits and routine, the worst number to look at is the one on the scale. When we change our bodies, our weight can and will fluctuate. It may dip and rise on a day-to-day basis. The last thing I want my patients to do is step on the scale in the morning and to see that the number has risen. This sets a tone of frustration and defeat, and it impacts the entire day.

Instead, what I ask my patients to do is first, ditch the scale and second, place the emphasis on the numbers that really matter. These numbers are the hours of sleep you are banking at night, the amount of hydration you achieve each day, the number of steps you take and the amount of time you allot for self-care and time with your family.

When it comes to nutrition, the philosophy of minor adjustments versus significant overhauls is the most effective way to create lasting change. I do not encourage people to go on drastic diets with all kinds of changes. When we do this, our brains revolt and remind us all day long about the foods we crave, how much we hate the new foods we are trying, and how hungry and miserable we are. The argumentative brain, combined with the lovely gastrointestinal issues that go along with dietary changes, really make for a fun day! Tomorrow will be a repeat of day one. This is no one's definition of fun.

What I do encourage is that my patients gradually change how and what they eat by simply taking one bite of what you know you should not eat off your plate and adding one bite of what you know you should eat. I like to joke that the bite added to your plate should be green—as in leafy green, not green Jell-O. As we subtly and gradually change what we eat, our brains adapt to this change and even eventually begin to crave the healthy foods. Over time, we change what we eat and adapt to new and healthier habits, which creates lasting change.

Sleep is a major issue for people who do shift work. Reporting for work early, working overnight, going to and returning from work when it is dark—all of these create disruptions to our circadian rhythms and disrupt our sleep. When it comes to building resilience, sleep is a significant goal we address.

Lack of sleep is a significant challenge to our mental health. Lack of sleep is associated with depression, anxiety, poor performance, weight gain, suicidal ideation, and interpersonal problems. The saying, "I'll sleep when I'm dead" should be changed to "I'll be dead sooner because I don't sleep."

The key is to bank enough time to get enough sleep. There is no exact number of hours for everyone in terms of what constitutes enough sleep, but the average goal is generally seven hours. Going to bed and getting up at the same time every day helps put us into a pattern or routine. Avoiding too much alcohol and caffeine are also good ways to enhance sleep. I encourage my patients to put their phones and tablets away about thirty minutes before it's time to go to sleep, and to definitely stay off social media before bedtime. Other ways to enhance sleep are to make your bedroom dark and cool, to declutter your bedroom, and to never fight with your spouse or significant other in the bedroom.

When people struggle to stay asleep, I teach them to allot about twenty minutes to fall back asleep after their brain has woken them up. If they are not able to fall back asleep after twenty minutes, I ask them to go ahead and get up, rather than tossing and turning helplessly. I encourage them to go to their living room and read or watch TV, but I ask them to sit up and focus versus leaning back in their favorite chair or lying on the couch. The act of sitting up and focusing on what they are doing is designed to wear them out faster. When they are starting to drift off, I instruct them to go back to bed and sleep. This teaches the brain that it is time to sleep when we are in bed. This does take several iterations to train the brain, but it works for many people.

After we begin working on the basics of resilience—hydration, nutrition, rest, and exercise—we then work in therapy on the next steps of resilience—family, friends, faith, and hobbies. In other words, your life outside of the job. Over time, the more we work and the more responsibilities we take on at work, the more work outweighs the rest of our lives.

As with the basics of resilience, I ask my patients to consider making small adjustments, so nothing feels too drastic. The simple act of taking fifteen minutes each day to breathe, read a book, or practice a hobby is how we start. Then we build on that.

One thing I explain to all my patients is that resilience is like a continuum, from low to high. Where you are on your continuum when the most stressful trauma occurs in your life does impact how you heal. If your resilience is high, and you are handed the worst call you have ever taken, you will be able to bounce back and heal much easier than if your resilience is low. Maintaining high resilience is a worthwhile endeavor.

As we make subtle changes in our lives, we start to realize and truly feel the impact of the changes being made. Our families notice this too. The analogy I give all first responders is that we all have an internal fuel tank. If public safety work drains the internal fuel tank, all first responders must spend their off-duty time refueling the internal fuel tank. This is done through resilience.

Trauma Care

Trauma treatment, and especially mitigation, is my absolute favorite thing about being a therapist. Whether a patient enters therapy with years of history to work through or jumps into therapy as soon as they realize they are not bouncing back from an event, helping my first responder patients heal is the absolute best job in the world. The main question I am asked is how I continue to treat so much trauma for so many years. My answer is two-fold: 1) I practice what I preach in terms of resilience, and 2) I see people heal, grow, and return to happy and healthy amazing human beings every day. Each patient who heals and succeeds motivates me to care for the next one.

My favorite modality for trauma is a combination of cognitive behavioral therapy (CBT), eye movement desensitization and reprocessing (EMDR) and progressive desensitization. Communications specialists benefit greatly from all three modalities.

Cognitive behavioral therapy aims to reduce anxiety and depression by challenging and changing cognitive distortions and improving emotional regulation. It also seeks to develop personal coping strategies. Doing CBT with clients involves unpacking the issues, examining and re-examining interpretations and reactions to these issues, and assigning homework to assist the client in approaching things and people differently.

EMDR is by far the best tool we have in the toolbox to combat trauma. Developed in the 1990s, EMDR replicates rapid eye movement, but the patient is obviously awake. In doing so, EMDR unlocks the trauma stored in the frontal lobe and moves it to long-term memory. As mentioned previously, we are now using EMDR early after a trauma, when it is still post-traumatic stress syndrome, in order to assure it does not become post-traumatic stress disorder.

The auditory trauma that communications specialists experience makes them great candidates for EMDR. My practice has had the privilege of working with so many dispatchers and 911 call takers and the impact of EMDR on their recovery is remarkable.

In my first book, *First Responder Resilience: Caring for Public Servants*, I describe what it's like when first responders experience EMDR:

> *The key to the EMDR process lies in the fact the brain is very resilient. EMDR is designed to process trauma; this technique taps into the brain's ability to heal itself. The process of replicating rapid eye movements triggers the frontal lobe to process those images and allows the brain to basically move them to long-term memory. The hippocampus generates new neural pathways in the process and actu-*

ally heals as it creates these new pathways to process trauma. The technique is fast and effective. It's exhausting and usually generates a headache, but when you think about the tremendous amount of work being done by a brain as it heals itself, grows new neural pathways, and unlocks and processes trauma, it's understandable that a patient is basically wiped out after an EMDR session. In addition to the images being processed, the emotions attached to the event get processed, as well. The beauty is that first responders don't have to talk about their feelings while this is occurring. They certainly can if they want to, but if it makes them uncomfortable, they don't have to. Bottom line: trauma and associated reactions get processed very quickly. First responders tell me all the time they wish they had done EMDR sooner, they now have their lives back, and that the treatment has been their pathway out of PTSD hell.

I was trained the original way in EMDR, which involves the patient tracking my fingertips as I move them back and forth in equal, bilateral motions, about twelve inches from the patient's face. Since its inception, EMDR has added light bars, pulse pads, and headphones with tones to mimic the bilateral stimulation and to help therapists with the arm fatigue many experience. The original method, as labor intensive as it can be, is still my favorite way to practice. While there are several steps we take throughout the EMDR process, I try to keep it as smooth and free-flowing as possible. You can read about the steps involved in the technique online or in any EMDR book. While I go through all these steps in every EMDR session, my goal is to keep first responders moving through each step, without troubling them with explanations. In other words, it's important to make the process seem more like a path or a journey that first responders and the clinician are taking together.

The outcome of the EMDR session is nothing short of amazing. When those synapses open and the brain starts to process the trauma, first responders tend to remember suppressed details. These are usually positive details, such as what they did to assist others.

Trauma is inherently negative—we always remember the bad—until we do EMDR. First responders also report that the pervasive, ugly images that have invaded their mind have faded. They describe the experience as gaining distance, fading, and even having a difficult time remembering it, or "seeing it," in their mind. The second part of this amazing process is the fact that patients will also notice that the very intense, negative emotions are gone. They describe being at peace with the event or just being "past it." As they discuss how they are responding so differently to the event after EMDR, they realize their perspective has changed. In other words, they usually realize they did everything they could in the situation or there was nothing more they could have realistically done. WOW!! For the first time ever after a trauma, first responders feel relief and they actually are able to forgive themselves.

After EMDR, I send my patients home for a nap, and I ask them to take it easy. They often note they are tired and report they sleep well through the night. Because we have opened the synapses and the brain is firing away, I explain to my patients that this processing will typically continue for a day or two. This means many events from their lives and careers will be reprocessed. The experience is that the images float by rapidly. I ask my patients to take note of the images, but to expect them to be gone very quickly. As a clinician, I always touch base with my clients the next day to see how they are doing and ask if they have any questions. I love hearing how significantly better they feel.

Progressive Desensitization

Progressive desensitization means going to the place where the trauma happened and overcoming any triggers or feelings associated with the event. I refer to EMDR followed by progressive desensitization as the one-two punch. I only do progressive desensitization after EMDR is completed, because the thought of revisiting the moment by going to the place where the event occurred before EMDR seems overwhelming, frightening, and impossible. After the trauma is processed and the triggers are diminished, progressive desensitization feels like a normal, progressive step in healing.

For communications specialists, progressive desensitization is slightly different. Based on the event and the way a dispatcher or 911 call taker is impacted, we implement progressive desensitization to fit their needs. One of my former patients was on duty the night her best friend was killed in an auto pedestrian accident, in the middle of the town where the dispatcher works. She was obviously very traumatized by this event. She came to therapy to work through both her grief and the trauma of being on duty as the 911 calls came in, eventually learning that the victim was her friend.

The location of the event occurred on a main road in town that the dispatcher normally took to work. As a result of this incident, the dispatcher created a seven-mile detour so that she could approach the police department from a different direction. This detour added forty minutes to her commute each way. Obviously, the loss of her friend was impacting her life in so many ways. No matter what she did, she felt as though she could not get control of things in her life.

Before I did EMDR on her, we talked about the progressive desensitization part of her therapy that would come later. She smiled at me and told me that seemed like a nice thought, but she was skeptical. We addressed the trauma of losing her friend during her EMDR. She was able to process the sounds of the callers from that night, as well as the shock of realizing who the victim was. At the end of EMDR she had such good fading, she could no longer hear the 911 calls that had invaded her mind since the event. After her EMDR, she told me she was ready to visit the scene.

The next day we drove to the scene. I first drove up and down the block a few times where her friend was killed. We talked the entire time about that night, about her friend, and about the aftermath of the event. Eventually we stopped and got out. We stood on the sidewalk and faced the road at the exact point she was hit. We talked and breathed together. At some point, the dispatcher looked at me and said, "I've got this." I asked her to drive her normal route to work the next day and to ditch the extra forty minutes she had added to her commute. The next day, she texted me that she had driven her normal route. "Mission accomplished" was what she said in her text.

Another former patient worked a horrendous line-of-duty death of a police officer. The entire situation was traumatic from start to finish, and by far this was the worst event she had experienced, not just at work, but in life. We did EMDR on the trauma from that night, and she returned to work. She noticed that certain words said on the radio and some specific calls were causing anxiety, and that when she was triggered it was hard to focus.

This dispatcher's progressive desensitization involved her direct supervisor and training scenarios. We worked to create a succession of situations that started mildly and became progressively worse. The supervisor was able to gradually turn the heat up and back off as needed to give this dispatcher time to process, get her confidence back, and return to her normal level of functioning. Once this was done, my patient was back on the radio, back in her groove, and confident once again.

Whenever possible, I like to have peer support team members help me with progressive desensitization. The reason is that peer support does the job, so they are very familiar with ways to help their colleagues get back in the saddle. Their wisdom and insight are such assets to this process.

Mindfulness and Breathing

The term mindfulness means moment-to-moment awareness of one's experience without judgment. Simply put, it means being in the moment. The goal of mindfulness is to achieve a state of alert, focused relaxation, which is achieved by paying attention to emotions, thoughts, and sensations.

When people are triggered by traumas, it is very difficult to stay in the moment. In an act of self-protection, the brain tells the body to launch into a fight-or-flight response, even when there is no danger present. Individuals who are traumatized frequently try to disconnect from triggers through dissociation, which is a disconnection and lack of continuity between thoughts, memories, actions, surroundings, and identity.

Breathing is also impacted by stress. When we are stressed, we hold our breath. When we are traumatized, we hold our breath. When we return to the place where the trauma occurred, we will frequently start holding our breath. Holding our breath is like bracing for impact. It's an act of self-protection and readiness. What actually happens, however, is we deprive our brains and bodies of oxygen, and it stresses our system even more.

As communications specialists heal from trauma, we reinforce the work we do in the therapy room by assigning mindfulness and breathing techniques. I try to keep mindfulness simple because I am usually asking a dispatcher or 911 call taker to practice this both on and off duty. I incorporate breathing and mindfulness at the same time because sometimes it's just easier to take a breath than to be mindful.

The typical assignment I will give a communications specialist is to do the following:

- When you enter the communications center, take a deep breath
- When you clock in, take a deep breath
- When you sit down at your console, take a deep breath
- When you sit down at your console, notice the chair under you and the floor under your feet (mindfulness)
- When the first call comes in, take a deep breath
- For every subsequent call, take a deep breath

- Notice the fan or air conditioner blowing (mind-fulness)
- Again, notice the chair under you and the floor beneath you (mindfulness)

Over time and with practice, communications specialists will notice that they are able to focus, maintain their presence, and even perform better. This is a tool that they frequently share with others, which is fantastic.

One of my former patients was extremely triggered one day in therapy. I asked her to notice my couch under her butt. She began to refer to mindfulness as "find your butt," and this is frequently how we refer to it in our practice.

Peer Support

Communications professionals are an inherently important part of any peer support program. I prefer that all areas of each department have peer support representation. Properly trained and coordinated peer support teams are an extremely important and valuable tool for departments to invest in.

As peer support teams activate for a situation, I am always grateful for the members who are looking after the communications folks and who are providing updates in terms of the needs of the communications center. I have noticed that in many callouts, the needs are very different from the field. There are times when the field is fine, but the call was horrendous from the communications stand-point, and vice versa.

In my book *First Responder Resilience: Caring for Public Servants*, I outline an effective way to manage group interventions. The acronym is TEN FOUR, and the process involves an educational piece by the peer support team, followed by an open discussion and then a focus on restoring resilience. When large-scale events dictate a group meeting, I always encourage the communications team to be present. I have witnessed so many discussions where the field had no idea what happened when the call first came in, and the communications team had no closure on the outcome. The ability to share this information is vital, as our brains want to fill in missing pieces of information in our minds. When we don't have the information, we often guess or assume. This does not enhance any closure and often leads to misperceptions and misunderstandings between communications and the field.

Meghan's Story

When departments open a position for a dispatcher in communications, you know you're expected to do certain things. They want you to be able to type 35 words per minute, they want you to be able to operate a computer system, monitor radio, and have amazing customer service skills.

But nowhere in the job description does it tell you that you will give up a piece of your soul to do the best job you can. They never tell you that in an instant your life can completely change, and your outlook of the world can completely shift. When you step foot on the floor of that communications center, you are no longer the person that you are outside that center. You are no longer a wife, a mother, a sister, a friend. You are a lifeline to every person you speak to, whether on the 911 phones, the administration lines, or that radio where you are the "calm in the chaos."

You will hear things that you can't unhear, you will handle situations that you never thought you were strong enough to handle. Then you will go home to sleep and come back to it again. Career communications is like a drug. Between the 911 calls and radio traffic, you begin to crave the chaos, request the hard assignments, and work the over- time because you want to be in the thick of it. As an emergency telecommunications officer, I have ex- perienced great things, such as helping a mother find her child, and I've experienced the worst things that humanity has to offer.

My worst day yet in my eleven-year career was March 31 at 2:43 in the morning. When my best friend Rowena Speight was murdered by her son, I took the call. You forever remember the dates and times of the calls that shape you. I picked up the 911 line and was immediately met with screams, and not just any screams. These were the visceral screams of a mother that had just lost her child. In those screams, I was able to recognize my best friend's mother's voice, and the only way that I knew to get her back, to break the hysteria thresh- old, was to call her "mom" because that's how I knew her.

Rowena's mom recognized my voice and said that Rowena was dead and that her son had killed her. I have never had a phone call cut so deep. It shook me to my core. My voice cracked as I continued to give her instructions, trying to get her to attempt CPR, to which she said, "She's gone."

By that time, we already had officers enroute to the location and EMS was staging. The medics got on scene and said that she was "not viable." Those two words would never hold the same meaning as they were used to describe my best friend. And even through all of this chaos, all of the pain, we had a job to do. We had to find her killer; we could be sad later, we could grieve the loss of the most amazing woman that had ever walked this earth later, but now we had a job to do.

Coordinating several agencies, getting K-9 on the ground, and helicopters in the air is a talented dance that takes your entire brain function to be able to accomplish. And if clouded by grief, you won't get the job done; you have to put your humanity aside, you have to put your feelings in a box so you can get this person who killed your best friend. The only thing going through my head the entire time was that I could be sad later, I could grieve later.

Officers were calling me, wanting to know what was going on. I told anybody who would listen that I was not leaving communications until he was found, and I made sure that he was in custody for murdering my best friend before I was able to go home. A fourteen-hour shift, and I felt every second of it. I had told my husband what happened earlier that night in a quick text message, as I didn't have time for anything else. I got home to a family that I had to tell that Rowena, who was my oldest daughter's surrogate grandmother, had been taken from us.

I came back on shift the next night to work so that my team didn't have to touch it, so they would not have to be in the yuck for one more night. I remember walking into the communications center and being hit with a wall full of flowers, which to me just smelled like a funeral home and reminded me of what I had just been through. I understand the sentiment that flowers show; it was just triggering. I remember when that 911 phone rang for the first time, my hand shook when I went to pick it up. It didn't shake for very long, but it was enough for me to remember that the last time that I picked up this phone was the call that changed my life. We were super fortunate because it was relatively slow the second night.

I remember having a few days off after that. It was Easter weekend, and we still hadn't bought our kids' Easter baskets. My husband drove me to a toy store to pick out our kids' Easter baskets and I just remember feeling this horrible anger inside. I didn't understand where it was coming from, just that I was so angry. My husband, who is an amazing man, couldn't see it. I just was so angry and exhausted at the same time. I was just trying to survive, but that wasn't good enough. I apparently needed to go pick out our kids' Easter baskets with him.

I remember being in the car and looking out the window and trying to close my eyes and forget that this horrible thing had happened. That didn't work. Every time I would close my eyes, I would hear those horrible screams; I would feel that horrible nausea like I was taking the call all over again. That's when I knew I was in trouble. The anger and exhaustion were overwhelming, and I needed to do something, but I couldn't figure out what to do. It was like being in the dark and desperately searching for a light switch, trying desperately to move forward, to adapt and overcome. This is what I was always taught—just keep swimming, just keep moving, and it will all be ok.

I remembered the post-incident meeting was on Friday, and I thought I could avoid the police department and not have to go to the meeting if I did. I picked up dinner for my family and realized that I had forgotten some paperwork that I needed for the next morning. I went into communications and picked up my paperwork and, as I was leaving, Tania was standing there. She told me that I was going to be at her office the next day for EMDR. I thought it was a complete bunch of "hooey" and didn't know why I needed it, except for when I saw Tania that night, everything came flooding back. The screams, nausea, and the exhaustion all came flooding in.

So, I went to Tania's office, and I sat on the couch, and she did EMDR and, quite frankly, it saved my life. I was able to sleep that night for the first time in I can't remember how many days. Tania also mentioned that I needed to get back to the gym not because I was overweight, which I am, but because mentally I needed it. I needed the stability that the gym provides. It started out slow. I started walking on the treadmill and then when I could walk a little faster, I would try to run and incorporate weights and different things. I found that's my sweet spot, my spiritual oasis.

I also did little things to lift my spirits. I open my curtains now every day to let the sunshine in, I make my bed because even if it's just one thing that I've accomplished for the day, that one thing sets me up on a positive note. I go to therapy once a week and Tania doesn't always tell me what I want to hear. She gives me the truth and that truth is that I did my job that night, that I'm not just a dispatch-er, I'm a badass.

This call could have broken me, I could have hung up my headset and never looked back. But that's not what Row would have wanted. She would have wanted me to continue to listen and to learn and to be the best dispatcher that I can be.

As dispatchers we are often forgotten, we are the unsung heroes, the chaos coordinators. We must be included as first responders. While we may not put on the vest, bunker gear, or stethoscope, we hear the screams of the helpless. We hear the cries for help and, after a while, it will wear on you.

Before communications, I was a paramedic in Flint, Michigan. I think that was easier, and I only say that because I at least had closure. I knew what had happened to the patient the majority of the time, and I did everything in my power to make sure the outcome was the best I could get. In communications, we don't have that luxury, we sometimes never know what happens. And more times than not, even if an award or accolade is given, communications is never recognized. It's part of the job to find the bad guy, even if we found him through a Facebook post he made with the motorcycle he just ran from officers with.

No one is saying we need a party every time we do something out of the box, because—let's face it—it would be a nonstop party. But recognition can go a long way. This is an ever-changing field with new and exciting things happening all the time. In the future, new technology could allow us to connect to callers visually and while that is exciting in some respects, it's terrifying in others.

I am living proof that seeking help will make you a better person. Allowing yourself to be vulnerable may not be the most fun thing you will ever do, but it will make you the best dispatcher that you can be. Know that you are never alone in this profession. You always have someone you can reach out to, even if it doesn't feel like it.

Meghan and Rowena

Chapter Five

The Path Ahead

An unforgotten tragedy
The answer isn't where you think you'd find it
Prepare yourself for this reckoning
"The Light" by Disturbed

The evolution of technology has been quite rapid in the last decade. Advances in equipment and systems have made the job of communications specialists more effective, efficient, and much faster. This has been a blessing in reducing errors, dispatch times, and call wait times.

There are new advancements on the horizon that I want to address in terms of communications resilience. With the latest advances in video capabilities and online meetings, the next trend in emergency communications will be video-style 911 calls.

In some areas, Next Generation 911 will replace existing narrowband, circuit-switched networks, which can only carry voice signals and very limited data, with new Internet Protocol-based networks that can carry a much wider range of data. In other areas, FirstNet is a new, nationwide public safety wireless communications network established by Congress in 2012, which in late 2017 became operational. NG911 and FirstNet are different systems moving on separate tracks, but they are complementary. Many police departments will implement both systems.

As its name implies, Next Generation 911 will eventually replace the current 911 system. NG911, as it is called, will allow people to send text messages, photos, videos, and other digital information to public safety.

This concept has its pros and cons. The best thing about the ability to use video, photos, and other digital information will be for the safety and well-being of the first responders in the field. Dispatchers who can see what is occurring, where it is occurring, how many weapons are present, etc., will be able to provide vital intelligence to the field as they respond. This will increase safety and most likely decrease misinformation and subsequent mistakes.

The negative aspect of this technology is the trauma that communications specialists will sustain. The events that individuals record and livestream can be quite traumatic. While communications specialists have traditionally dealt with the information and the auditory trauma, the visuals will add an additional layer of trauma.

In my practice, we receive numerous calls each month from the parents of young adults who work in the field of social media, and whose job it is to monitor and censor content. The parents are frequently desperate to find a trauma therapist who can help their children because they see the way some of the horror they are exposed to is changing them.

If this is the way of the future, then we must prepare. Step one in preparation is training. Communications academies and training programs will need to prepare personnel for what they are about to endure by desensitizing them. Students will need to see these types of videos, starting on the mild end of the spectrum in terms of trauma and increasing gradually to worse and worse. Instructors will be charged with monitoring the students and allowing them to process what they are seeing. Competent instructors will be able to normalize the experience without condoning the violence. At each step of the way, communications trainers must ensure that students are becoming progressively desensitized while not losing their empathy or humanity and ensuring that students are not developing maladaptive responses to the traumas they are witnessing. The worst-case scenario is that communications specialists emerge from training with post-traumatic stress disorder.

When we look at any high-stress occupation, whether it's public safety or the military, no one starts at their highest skill level. Everyone starts with the basics and develops skills, strength, stamina, and tolerance to pain or adversity. The same will need to occur for communications specialists.

During CPR training one year, I asked why the class instruction never mentions how it feels when ribs crack from chest compressions or how sometimes people vomit or lose control of their bladder or bowel during CPR. I was told that for the public, the concern is if you mention those things, people will hesitate to perform CPR. So, the practice is to not warn them but run the risk of traumatizing them.

When I started working with a commercial airline in 2002, I noticed that a lot of flight attendants were struggling with the aftermath of CPR for this very reason. I approached the training division with the help of the head of the peer support team and outlined my concerns. Flight attendants must perform these duties, especially if there are no medical personnel on board a particular flight who can assist. They may have to perform CPR on passengers several times throughout their careers, so traumatizing them the first time and hoping they can perform CPR a second time seemed like an inadequate plan. The trainers agreed and completely changed over to a new training style with as much information as they could provide to warn the flight attendants of what to expect. The post-CPR traumas for flight attendants dropped significantly after the training changed.

Step two in preparation for the onset of video 911 calls is trauma care. In Chapter Four, I addressed what I consider the best standards for trauma care, but if the new generation of 911 calls involves videos, the industry should add even more tools for employee care.

The first area to address is the culture of the communications center and supervisory oversight of the level of trauma that communications personnel experience. In other words, supervisors should be tracking the content and truly assuring that communications specialists are psychologically intact after a bad call. While this should be going on anyway, if video 911 calls are introduced, it is a must that this takes priority.

Sometimes after bad calls, communications specialists benefit from words of encouragement from supervisors or peers. Sometimes they need to take a break and walk around for a bit or call their loved ones. Other times, they may need to get off the floor and either go do something else for the rest of the shift or go home. Forcing someone to remain on the floor after they are completely traumatized will only exacerbate their trauma.

The establishment of robust, competent peer support teams for communications professionals is another important part of the care continuum. Having peers in place to check on their colleagues after horrendous calls, to assure that personnel are bouncing back after witnessing horrendous videos and making sure that the bridge to professional care is occurring when dispatchers and 911 call takers are not healing, is a proactive way to embrace the trauma that communications specialists are facing and to assure their healthy recovery.

Another important component is the access to competent mental health professionals to assist as needed. One of my customers is a state law enforcement agency. Within the agency is a child exploitation unit (CEU). These officers investigate child sexual assault material daily. It takes a very special person to do this job, and they are amazing people.

About five years ago, the agency brought me on to not only assist with critical incidents, but to care for the hearts and minds of the CEU. I started with training, as I always do, which addressed the physical and psychological responses to stress, as well as solutions for trauma. I began to meet with each officer every six months. Initially, they were very skeptical. I made it clear that in no way was I there to jeopardize their careers and that they did not have to say anything they were not comfortable with.

Over time, each officer opened up more. They are now at the point where they will make appoint-

ments in between the six month scheduled appoint-
ments and any time they feel as though they need to
offload the trauma. While the agency makes the
semi-annual visit mandatory, it really has just become a thing that everyone does. I have noticed that
new members of the CEU come in with much less
resistance because they are told about this benefit
during their onboarding, and apparently the existing
team members speak highly of it.

I firmly believe that if communications specialists are going to witness crimes in progress via
video, this is one of the best and most productive
ways to help them. Go offload the "yuck" every six
months, and more often if you want to. And by the
way—everyone does it, so there is no stigma. This
is a perfect way for communications specialists to
get help without the anxiety of having to ask for it.

The clinicians who do this work need to be
hand-picked and specially trained. They need to
have strong backgrounds in trauma work and should
spend some time under a headset before they start.
This is not a simple "call the EAP" protocol, as this
will not suffice for the needs of communications
specialists exposed to this level of trauma.

As communications centers lean into the next generation of technology, I strongly encourage leadership to get ahead of the problems the technology will create by leaning into and investing in great training and mental health care for communications specialists. It's the right thing to do at the right time. After all, where would we be without our dispatchers and 911 call takers?

In Closing

I have been so honored to work with many communications specialists in my career, and I am excited for what's ahead as we continue to refine trauma treatment and place enough emphasis on assisting our heroes under the headset. I thank you for what you do, and I wish you all the best. You are loved.

About the Author

Tania was three months from completing her master's degree at the University of Texas when she witnessed the dramatic and violent standoff between law enforcement and the Branch Davidian cult in Waco, Texas. At that point, she knew her calling was to work with first responders and focus on healing these warriors from the horrors of post-traumatic stress disorder.

Tania spent the first ten years of her career working in a Level II Trauma Emergency Department on weekends as she built her private practice during the week. In 2002, Tania transitioned to her private practice on a full-time basis and has dedicated her entire career to working with first responders and military members.

Tania assisted with the aftermath of the Oklahoma City Murrah Federal Building bombing, the 9/11 attacks on the World Trade Center, Hurricane Katrina, the Dallas Police shootings, and numerous other incidents. She is referred to as the "warrior healer" by her colleagues, and she is passionate about her work. Tania resides in Central Texas. Her loves include her family, her pets, and fitness nights. For more information, please contact Tania at www.taniaglenn.com.

Tania has seven other books published by Progressive Rising Phoenix Press:

First Responder Resilience: Caring for Public Servants

Protected But Scared

Code Four: Surviving and Thriving in Public Safety

First Responder Families: Caring for the Hidden Heroes

Smashing the Stigma and Changing the Culture in Emergency Services

I've Got Your 6: Peer Support for First Responders

This Is Our Normal